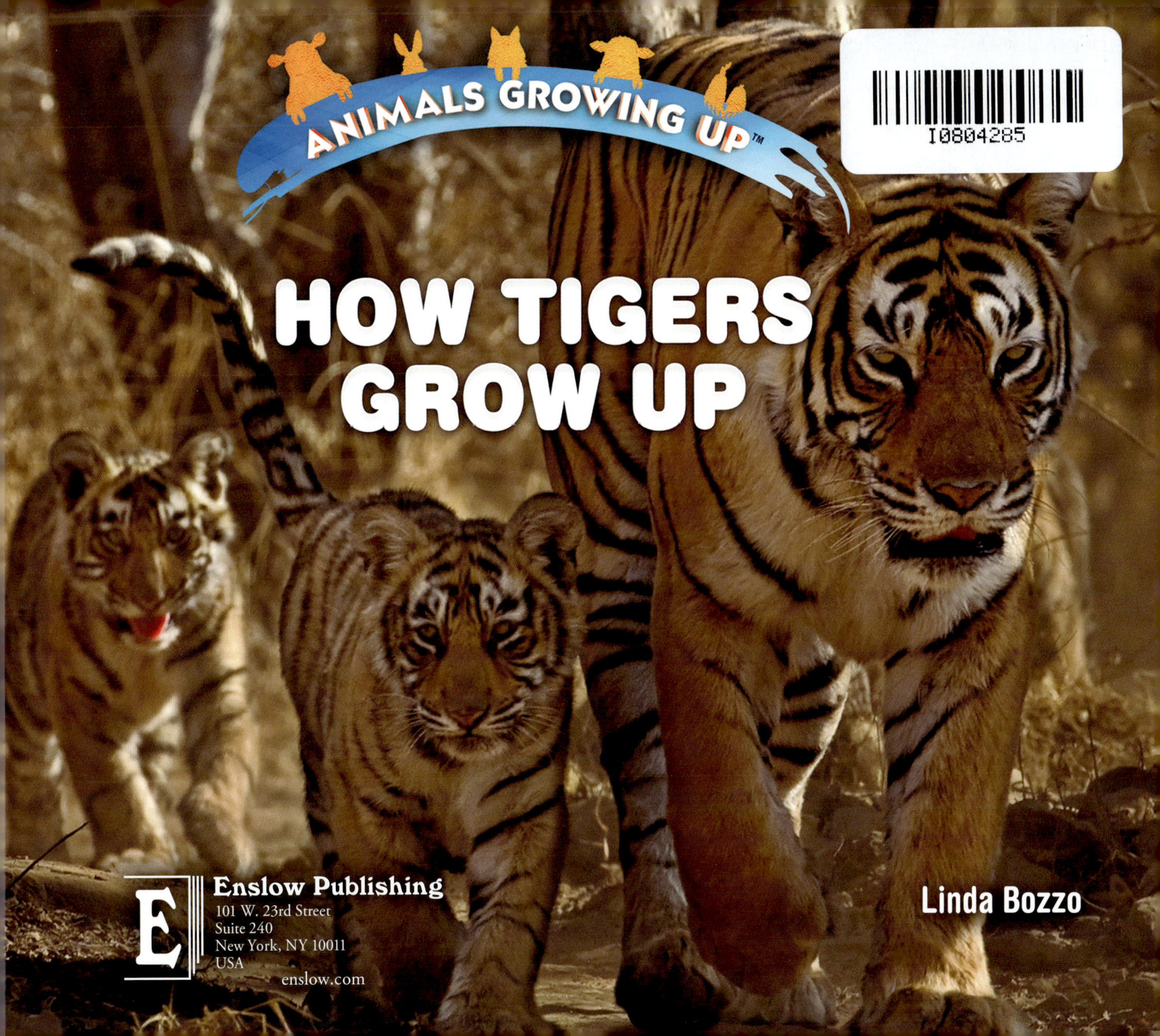

ANIMALS GROWING UP™

HOW TIGERS GROW UP

Linda Bozzo

Enslow Publishing
101 W. 23rd Street
Suite 240
New York, NY 10011
USA
enslow.com

I0804285

WORDS TO KNOW

cubs Baby tigers.

den A place where the mother tiger gives birth and raises her cubs.

habitats Places in which plants and animals live.

litter A group of animals born at the same time to one mother.

mammals Warm-blooded animals that breathe air, have backbones and hair, and produce milk for their young.

predators Animals that kill and eat other animals to live.

prey An animal that is killed and eaten by another animal.

territory A large area of land.

CONTENTS

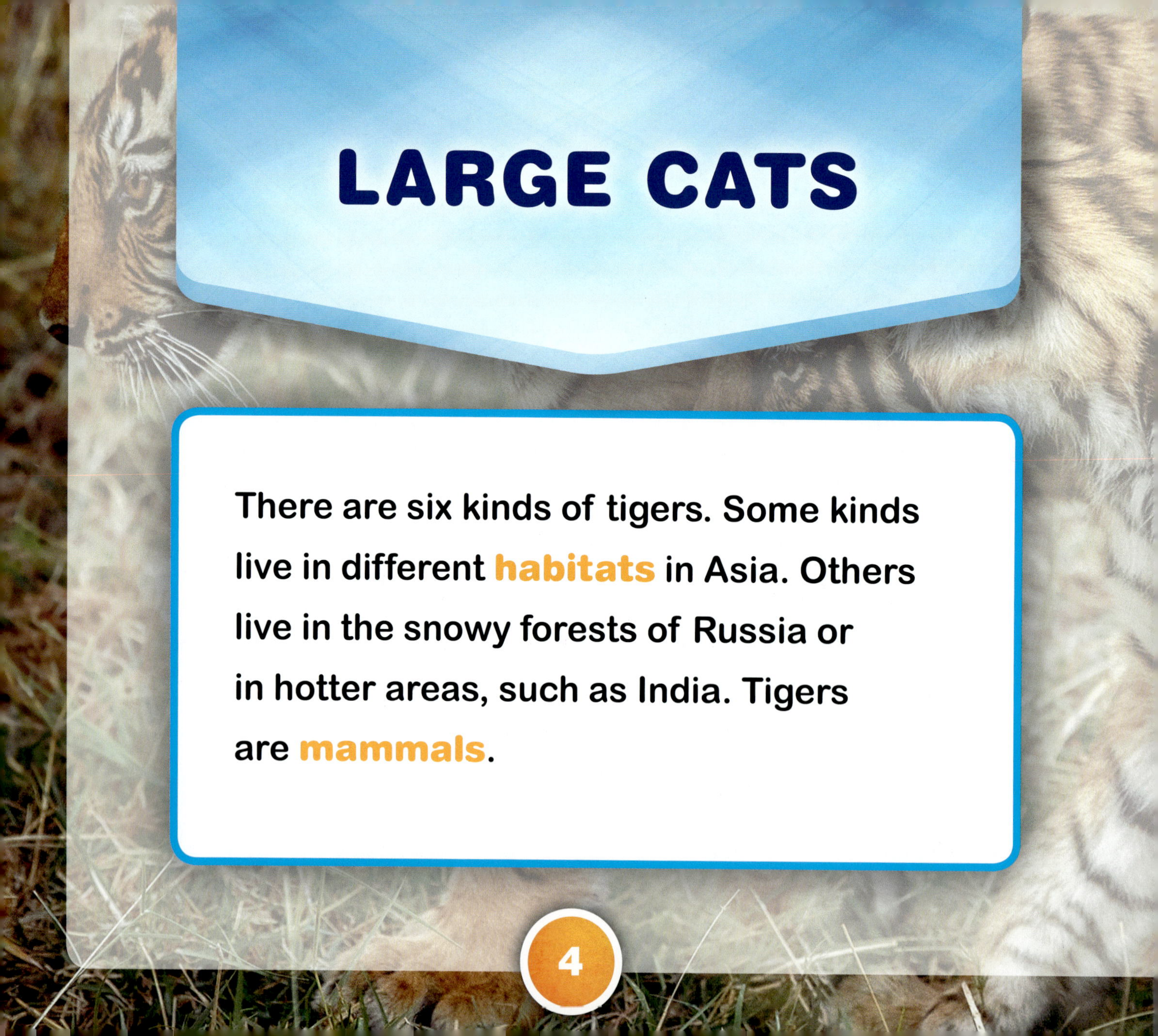

LARGE CATS

There are six kinds of tigers. Some kinds live in different **habitats** in Asia. Others live in the snowy forests of Russia or in hotter areas, such as India. Tigers are **mammals**.

FAST FACT

The Siberian tiger is the largest cat in the world. It lives in Siberia, a part of Russia.

A mother Siberian tiger licks her baby.

TIGER CUBS

Baby tigers are called **cubs**. A **litter** of tiger cubs are born in a **den**. A den can be inside a cave, a large tree, or in tall, thick bushes. Each litter may have three or four cubs.

These are newborn white Bengal tiger cubs.

FAST FACT

Tiger cubs are born with their eyes closed.

ENOUGH FOOD

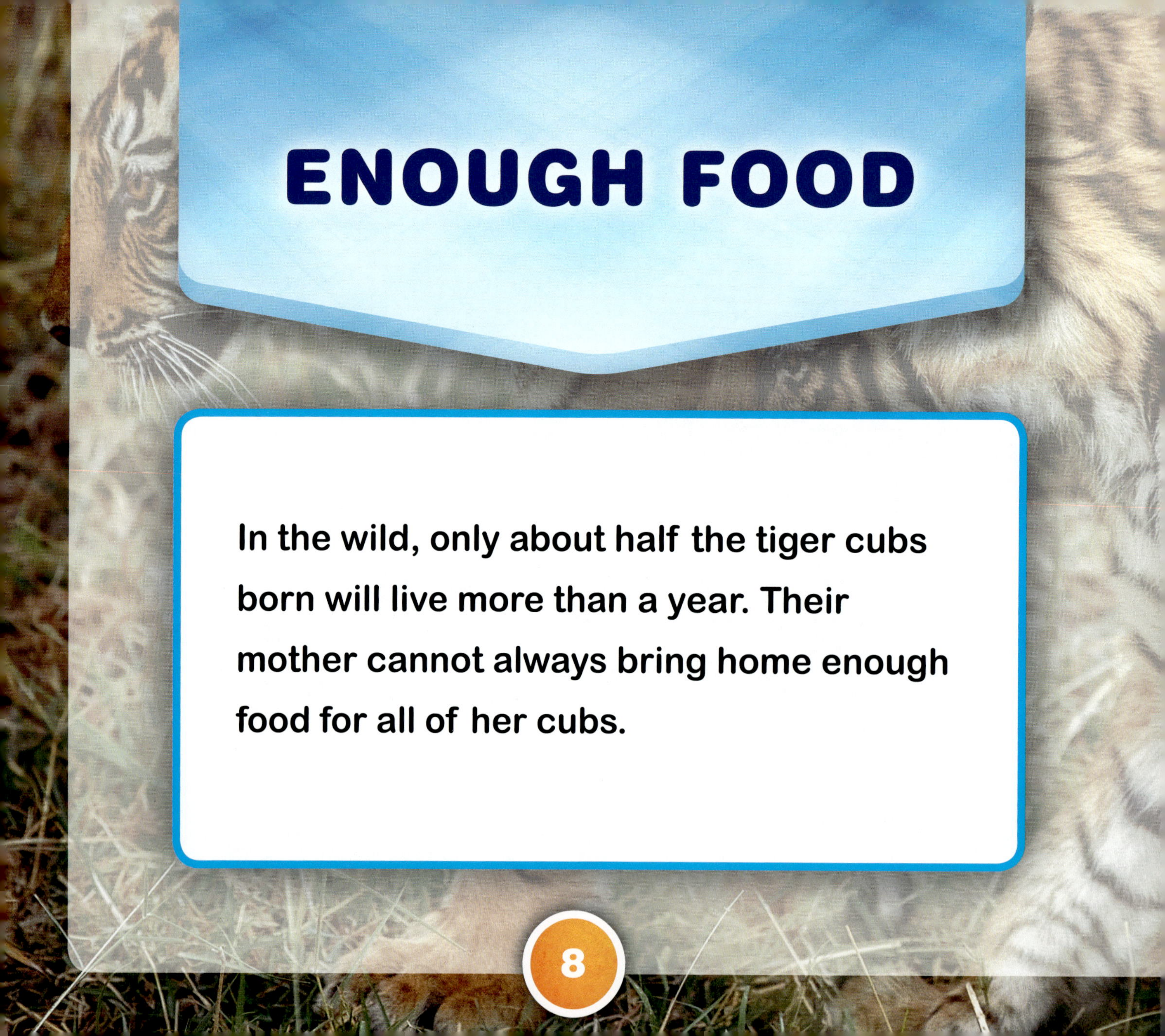

In the wild, only about half the tiger cubs born will live more than a year. Their mother cannot always bring home enough food for all of her cubs.

FAST FACT

At first, cubs will drink milk from their mother. Later, they will eat meat.

All mammals drink milk from their mothers, like these tiger cubs do.

FIRST LOOK

Tiger cubs grow very fast. Soon they start to leave their den with their mother. They must look out for **predators** such as wild dogs and other tigers.

FAST FACT

Tigers can run, swim, or even climb trees to escape an enemy.

Tigers are very good swimmers. Sometimes cubs must swim to safety.

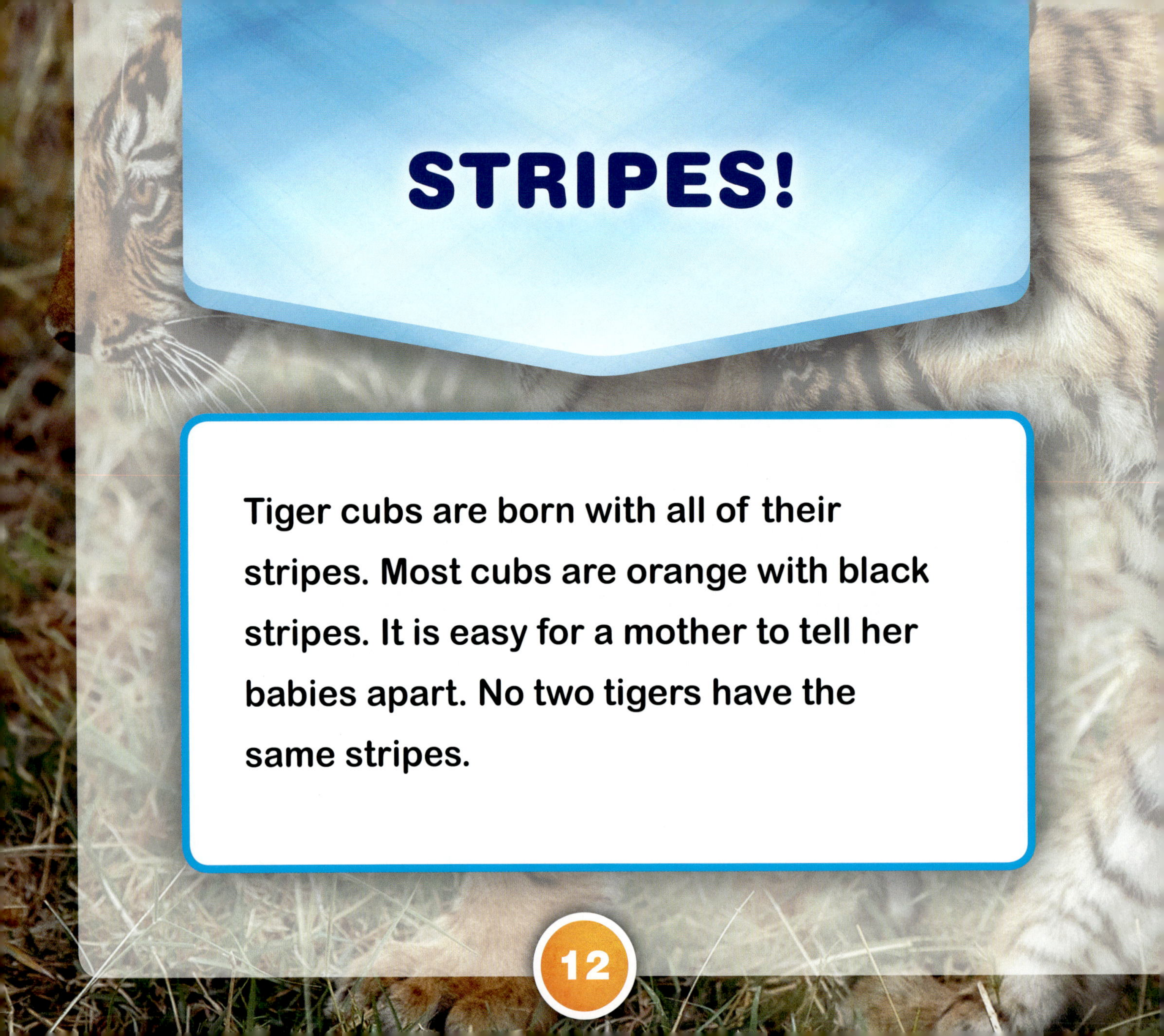

STRIPES!

Tiger cubs are born with all of their stripes. Most cubs are orange with black stripes. It is easy for a mother to tell her babies apart. No two tigers have the same stripes.

FAST FACT

A tiger cub's striped fur helps keep it hidden in the tall grass.

These cubs are Sumatran tigers. They live on the island of Sumatra in Indonesia. Indonesia is in Asia.

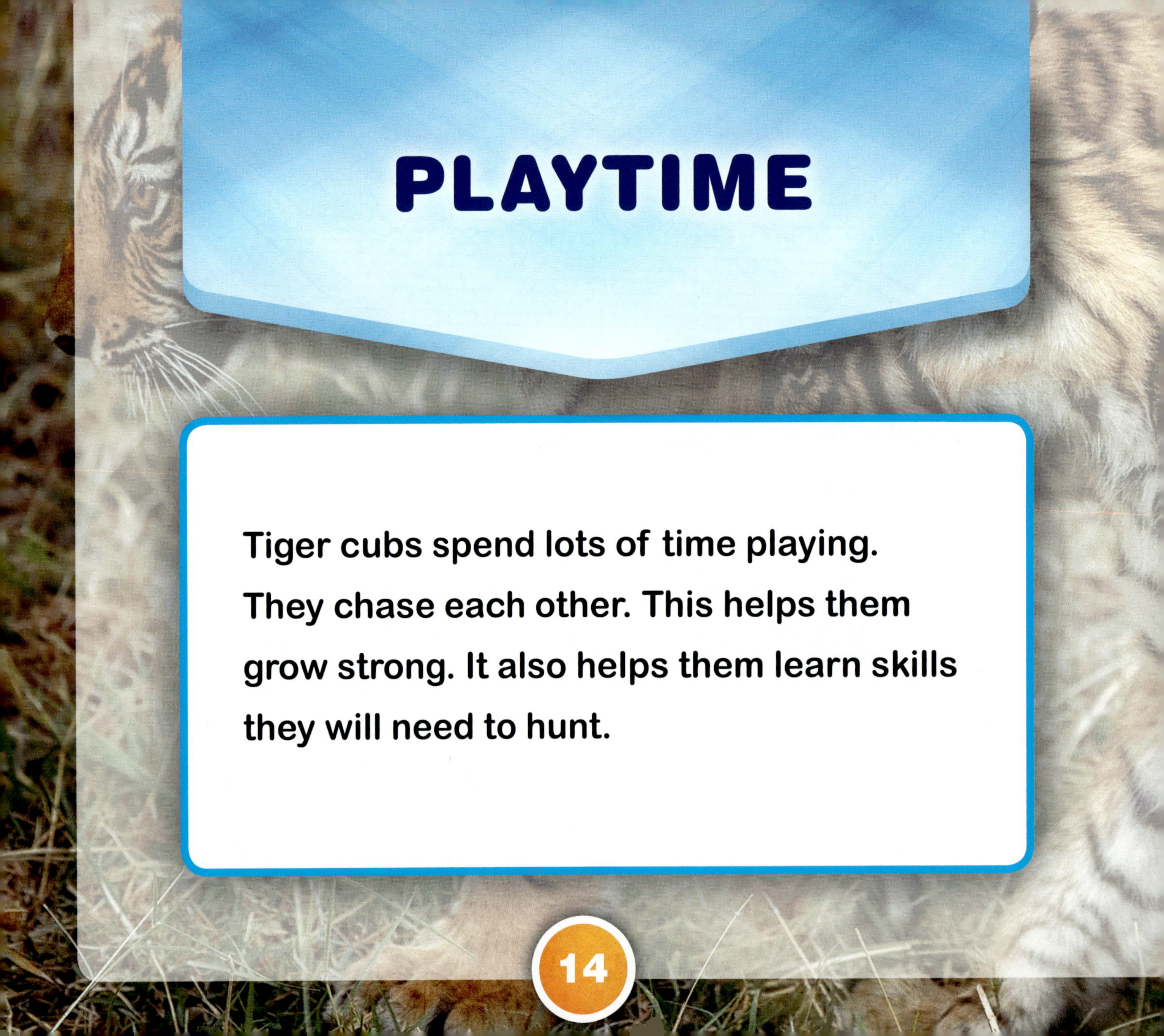

PLAYTIME

Tiger cubs spend lots of time playing. They chase each other. This helps them grow strong. It also helps them learn skills they will need to hunt.

FAST FACT

Tiger cubs play fight to practice their hunting skills.

These Siberian tiger cubs may be part of the same litter, but they still fight!

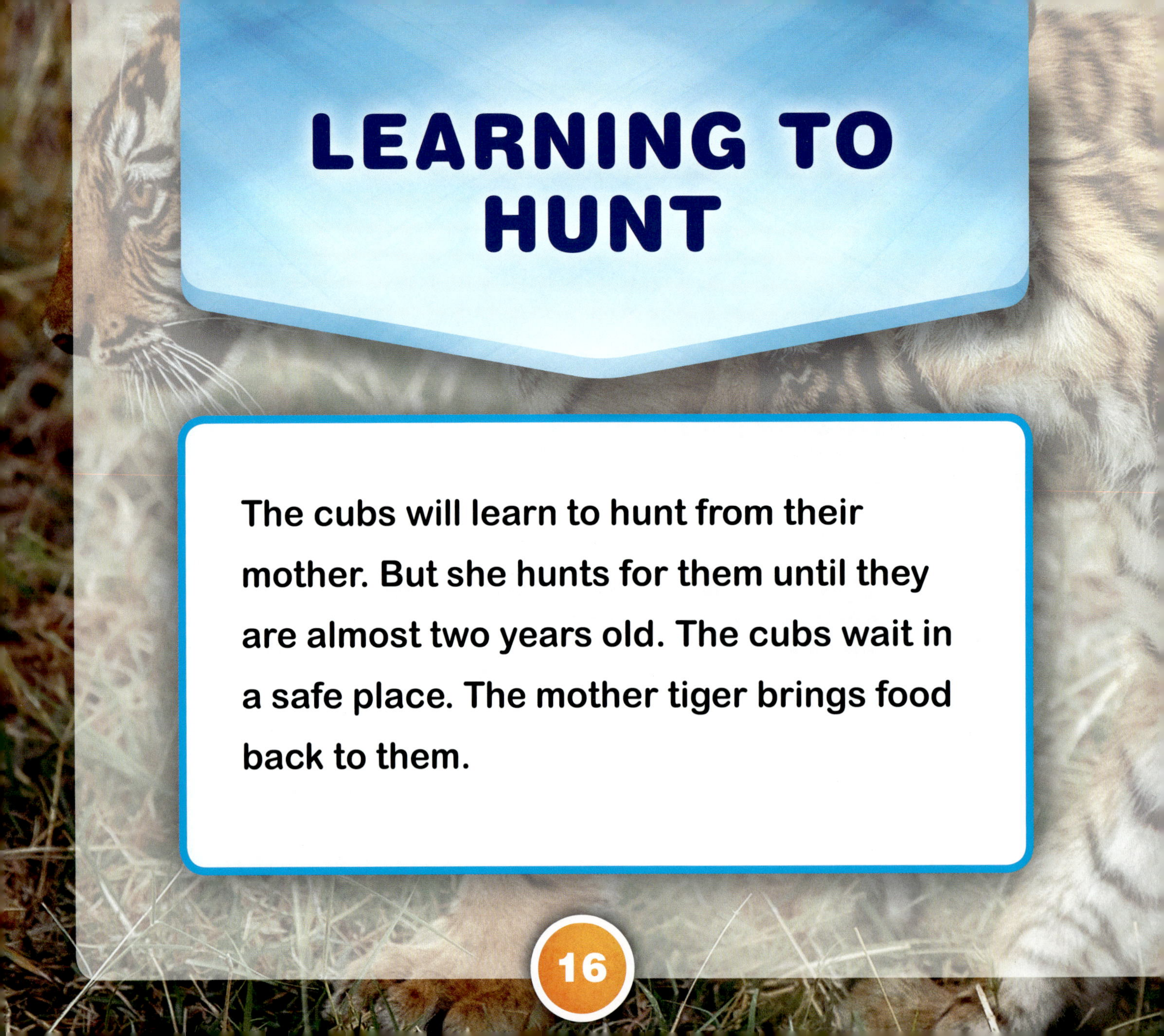

LEARNING TO HUNT

The cubs will learn to hunt from their mother. But she hunts for them until they are almost two years old. The cubs wait in a safe place. The mother tiger brings food back to them.

Tiger cubs wait for their mother to bring them back some meat.

FAST FACT

A tiger can eat up to 60 pounds (27 kg) of meat at one time.

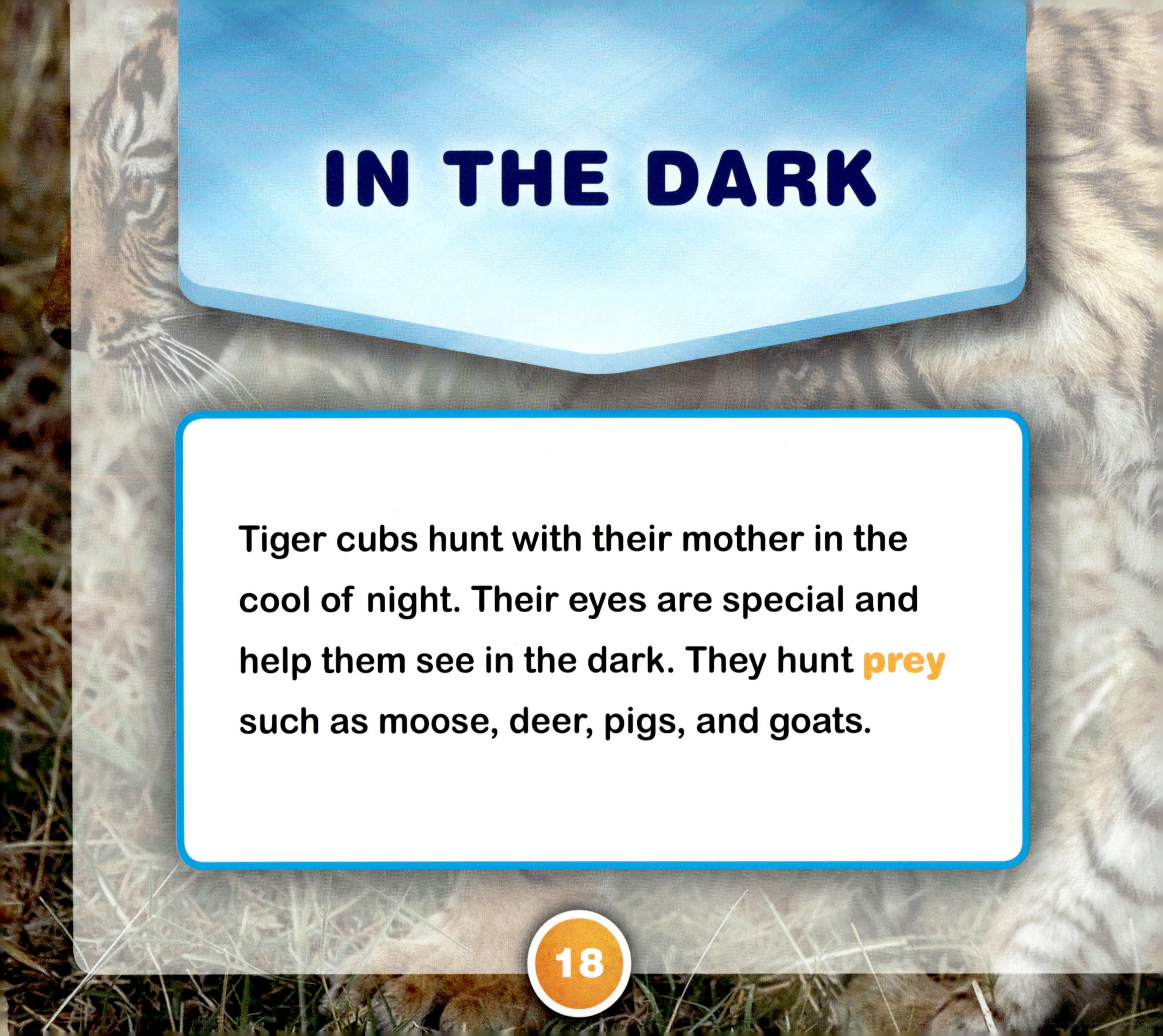

IN THE DARK

Tiger cubs hunt with their mother in the cool of night. Their eyes are special and help them see in the dark. They hunt **prey** such as moose, deer, pigs, and goats.

FAST FACT

Sometimes tigers eat grass, fruit, and berries to help their stomachs.

Like other predators, a tiger's eyes are on the front of its head. This helps it figure out how close or far prey is.

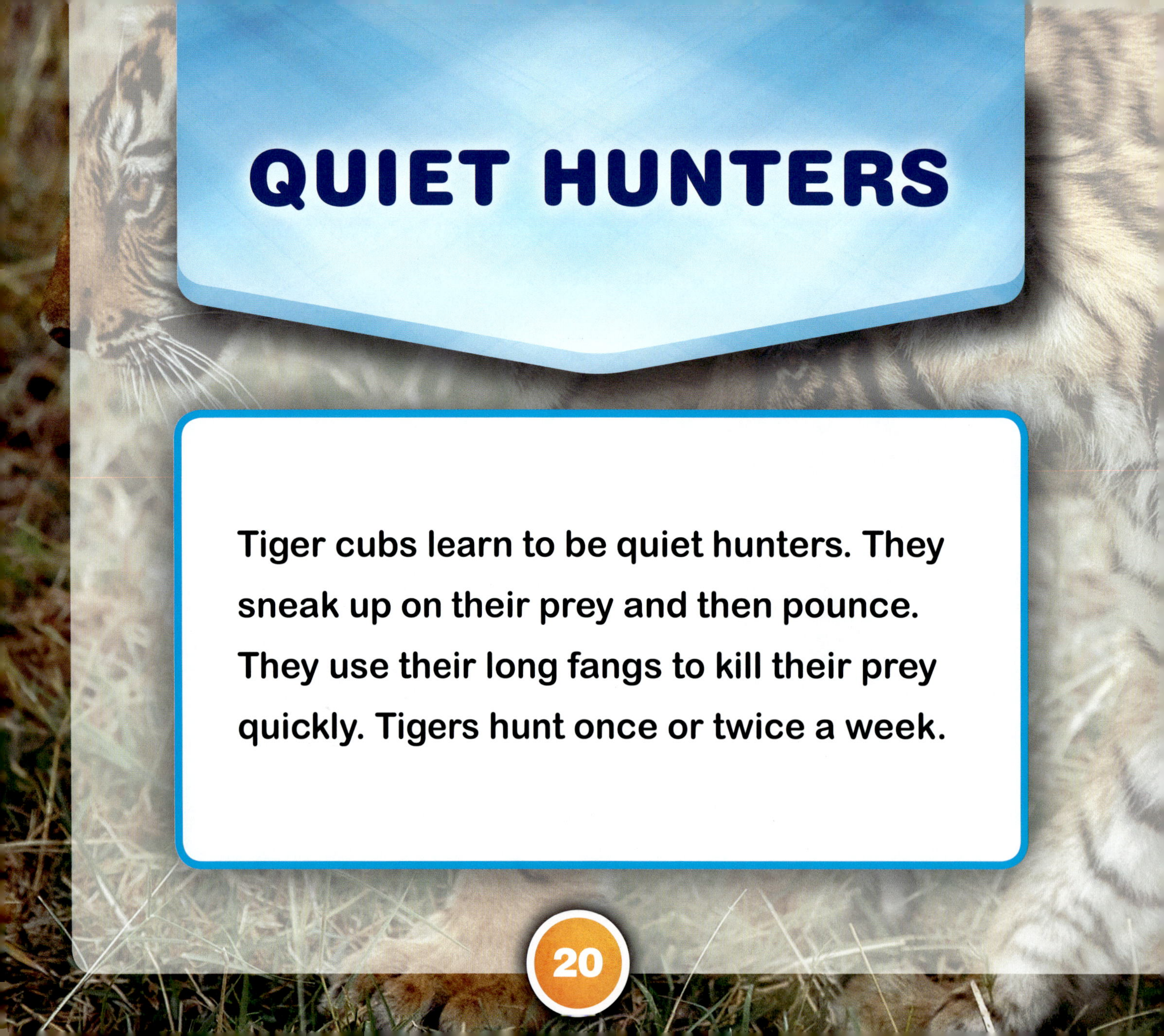

QUIET HUNTERS

Tiger cubs learn to be quiet hunters. They sneak up on their prey and then pounce. They use their long fangs to kill their prey quickly. Tigers hunt once or twice a week.

A tiger cub enjoys fresh meat from a hunt.

FAST FACT

Tigers bury their leftovers. They snack on them for the next few days.

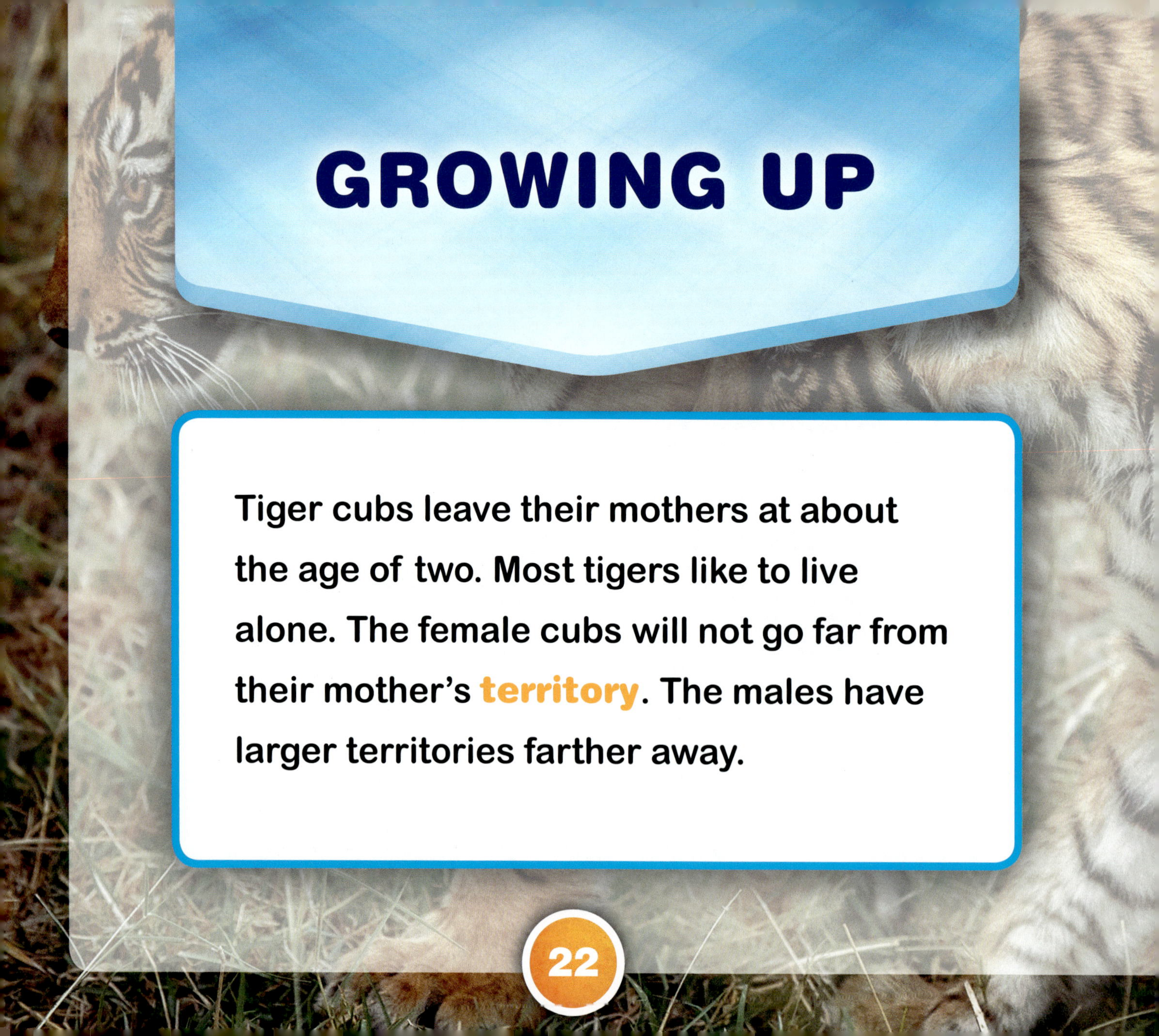

GROWING UP

Tiger cubs leave their mothers at about the age of two. Most tigers like to live alone. The female cubs will not go far from their mother's **territory**. The males have larger territories farther away.

FAST FACT

Tigers have been known to live up to 20 years in the wild.

A young tiger sets off to find its own home.

LEARN MORE

Books

Brannon, Cecelia H. *Baby Tigers at the Zoo*. New York, NY: Enslow Publishing, 2017.

Kelley, K. C. *Baby Tigers*. Mankato, MN: Amicus, 2018.

Shafer, Barbara. *Baby Tigers*. Chicago, IL: World Book, Inc., 2019.

Websites

National Geographic Kids: Tiger
kids.nationalgeographic.com/animals/tiger/
Learn how this powerful predator hunts.

San Diego Zoo Kids: Tiger
kids.sandiegozoo.org/animals/tiger
Read more facts about tigers.

INDEX

Published in 2020 by Enslow Publishing, LLC
101 W. 23rd Street, Suite 240, New York, NY 10011

Copyright © 2020 by Enslow Publishing, LLC.

All rights reserved.

No part of this book may be reproduced by any means without the written permission of the publisher.

Library of Congress Cataloging-in-Publication Data

Names: Bozzo, Linda, author.
Title: How tigers grow up / Linda Bozzo.
Description: New York : Enslow Publishing, 2020. | Series: Animals growing up | Audience: K to Grade 3. | Includes bibliographical references and index.
Identifiers: LCCN 2019010457| ISBN 9781978512511 (library bound) | ISBN 9781978512498 (paperback) | ISBN 9781978512504 (6 pack)
Subjects: LCSH: Tiger–Development–Juvenile literature. | Tiger–Infancy–Juvenile literature.
Classification: LCC QL737.C23 B697 2020 | DDC 599.75613/92–dc23
LC record available at https://lccn.loc.gov/2019010457

Printed in the United States of America

To Our Readers: We have done our best to make sure all website addresses in this book were active and appropriate when we went to press. However, the author and the publisher have no control over and assume no liability for the material available on those websites or on any websites they may link to. Any comments or suggestions can be sent by email to customerservice@enslow.com.

Photos Credits: Cover, p. 1 © iStockphoto.com/dickysingh; interior pages 4-23 (background), p. 17 Mark_Kostich/Shutterstock.com; 5. Tambako the Jaguar/ Moment/Getty Images; p. 7 © iStockphoto.com/anankkml; p. 9 Terry Whittaker/ Corbis NX/Getty Images; p. 11 © Renee Lynn/VCG/Corbis Documentary/ Getty Images; p. 13 Schafer & Hill/Stone/Getty Images; p. 15 Ronald Wittek/ Photographer's Choice RF/Getty Images; p. 17 PhotocechCZ/Shutterstock.com; p. 19 Helen E. Grose/Shutterstock.com; p. 21 Ewa Studio/Shutterstock.com; p. 23 kyslynskahal/Shutterstock.com; back cover and additional interior pages background graphic 13Imagery/Shutterstock.com